Divining
Moments

Jackie Choquette Picard

~Hallowed Abyss LTD~

Published by **Hallowed Abyss, LTD**

Rhode Island

REVIEWS

These simple, yet profound stories remind us that God is present and found in the most ordinary circumstances of our daily life. The memories that the author recounts will speak to each reader in their own unique way, helping all of them see how their own experiences can reveal God's presence in their life. Jackie Picard has provided us with a rich source for reflection and prayer.

Francesco C. Cesareo Ph.D. President, Assumption College

These "moments," so well written, teach us the beauty of selfless love, of self-surrender, and oneness with Him, and openness, so that He can teach others through us. Jackie's writing illustrates her convictions. Her love of God and all beings, and her ability to recognize Him in everyone is visibly clear, as is the breadth and depth of her immersion in life and love, and her willingness to share that with whoever will engage. These stories resonate like crystal amidst the din and noise of modern culture.

Jim and Kathy Brennan

Remarkable stories from a remarkable life. These snapshots of discovering the divine moments in everyday life are equal parts heartfelt, delightful, thought-provoking and moving.

Brady Dennis, staff writer, *The Washington Post*

Jackie Picard has given all of us a most rare and refreshing book in her lively and lovely witness to God's presence in her life. What is particularly refreshing about "Divining Moments" is the fact that it opens a door to each one of us and beckons us to live in that space where we not only look for God but expect God to be there, reaching out to us in immense love and profound personal care. As you read, I believe you will not only rejoice in Jackie's experiences, you will also be drawn to recognize God's ways in your own life, and to be deeply grateful for them. You may even be inspired to jot them down as she has done, that at least those near and dear to you will know, as she puts it, "Every individual one of us is the absolute apple of His eye!"

Maureen McCabe, O.C.S.O., Abbess of the Cistercians in Wrentham, MA

REVIEWS

The reader of "Divining Moments" is blessed with such a wealth of experience, wisdom, and awe on these pages. The powerful sense of the writer's gratitude to God is the unmistakable motif that ties them together, delivered in the author's quirky, self-deprecating, ebullient, discerning-but-never-preachy voice. Jackie is our lively tour guide on this journey and we experience with her, these moments of grace.

John Guevremont, Mount St. Charles Academy

CONTENTS

CONTENTS

CONTENTS

FOREWORD

What I want to do here is set down for my own satisfaction, all the times in my life that I can remember when God has reached out, Personally, to make contact with me. Does that sound like a bit of self-aggrandizement to you? Not surprising. I felt the same way myself, at first, but I truly do believe now that He does that with every human being, all through his/her life. I think more than anything, He wants to get our attention, so that we can come to realize the incredible connection between us. Between Him—unquestionably the highest, and greatest Power in the universe—and every single person on this earth! If you're open to that possibility, and paying attention in any way, He'll come through, and life will get to be fascinating. If you're not connecting at all, and not interested, you'll never even know He's real, and trying to reach you...or how much He loves you. I didn't appreciate His amazing involvement in my life until my later years, but this new awareness made me want to help people recognize and *feel* that love themselves. What a difference it will make in your life when you know it to be true for you.

I started collecting the anecdotes, and fleshing them out, but then this other thought entered my head. If I wanted to leave a legacy of sorts to my children, grandchildren, and great-grands (and you, too, reading this, whoever you are!) what better way to communicate with you all than to share the stories of God in my life, that I found most compelling. All these incidents made me realize how much I—and you—and every individual one of us—is the absolute apple of His eye! These were life-altering moments for me, and as I look back, I see how they shaped my living and my loving and are making me whatever I'll finally turn into. (I'm not there yet!)

1

Anyway, I have a whole assortment of episodes. Some are crucial, and without His obvious intervention, our lives would have been disastrously different. In others, a timely little nudge from Him turned despair into delight…and some, that might seem totally insignificant to you, just made me more conscious of His caring. Other God-experiences, long buried in my subconscious, keep surfacing every now and then. It's engaging. I'm hoping they all make it to this book.

I'm also hoping these stories will somehow spur you to look for the Divining Moments in your *own* lives. They'll identify you as His, and help you come to realize for yourselves, whole-heartedly, how much *you* matter!…*as does every single one of us!*… to the Master Mind of the entire cosmos, the very same Being who created us and loves us unfathomably.

RUBY RING

How old was I, I wonder? Probably anywhere between five and seven, and it was actually very exciting…

To begin with, a new ruby ring had to be exciting! We weren't a "jewelry" family by any means, not even at Christmas time, but this year was different. And there it was, on my ring finger, left hand, my own beautiful brand-new ring! It was Sunday morning, and we were at St. John the Baptist Church for Mass. As I'm admiring my new possession, Jesus appeared to me, right on it!

Had I been expecting Him? I don't know, but the nuns at school often told us that Jesus appeared to His saints, asking for their whole-hearted commitment. This was what He was asking me: Would I say "yes" forever? Was I willing to be a saint? To be His? I remember being in awe of having Him appear to me. (The nuns must have done their work well!) Anyway, to the Jesus with the brown beard, in a scarlet robe, proposing to me from the ruby ring on my own finger, and waiting for my response to His invitation, incredible as it all was, I solemnly whispered the promise to be, to do…whatever. I remember no specifics. The answer was just clear: "Yes."

But wait—while I was musing on what just happened, He disappeared. Oh well, I didn't expect His image to be permanently affixed to my stone, but suddenly—there He was, again! To my profound amazement, it came to me that I could control His coming and going at will. As I looked around, I realized that the Jesus who courted me bore a striking resemblance to the Jesus who stood with the apostles by the shore of Galilee, in the rich stained-glass window on the right side of our church. It took just a minute for a bright little peanut to figure it out. Did the bubble burst? Did I feel deceived and deflated? Hoodwinked, by my own hand? Oddly enough, in answer to all those questions, "No, not a bit." The proposal had been heard and accepted. What difference did it make that there was a natural explanation? Again, *surprisingly* to me, none whatsoever!

It was a sweet and gentle introduction to the matter of miracles.

A SPECIAL REMEMBRANCE

There were five of us growing up together on Pleasant Street. A happy bunch and only very rarely was there a sense that you were part of a herd. My younger sister Pauline and I (17 months apart) shared a room, and a double bed. One night, (I might have been six) my mom came into our room, long after we'd gotten tucked in. "How come you're still wide awake?" she asked. "I don't know, I'm not sleepy," I replied. "Well, would you like to come downstairs with Daddy and me for a little while?" she questioned. She was offering me uniqueness! ...wholeness!...singular glory! I hardly dared breathe lest I wake my sister. This magic moment was *not* to be shared. Gingerly and motionless almost, I slid out from beneath the covers, put on my slippers and tiptoed victoriously from the room.

Descending those navy-blue carpeted stairs by myself, I felt every inch a queen. The memory of it still glows. I was not a princess, but a queen. At every downward step, (my image being reflected in the gold-framed mirror that faced the stairs,) that impression was indelibly imprinted on my psyche. It wasn't as if I were a guest of honor there though, either. Not by any means. My dad hardly looked up from his newspaper. My mother was busy with the sewing in her lap. Neither one paid much attention to me. No matter. I just sat there on the sofa against the window-wall, relishing the sensation that this night, like no other, was mine! It was thrilling.

A few years later I was confiding this dearest memory to my older sister, Muriel, (better known as Tootsie or Toots) when she interrupted: "You made this up. That sofa was never against the wall with the windows." "Yes it was," I protested vehemently. " I know where I was sitting!" We argued back and forth and then she said: "Let's just ask Mom, she'll know." In response to Tootsie's question, my mother confirmed that the sofa had always been on the side wall facing the fireplace. "Mom," I wailed, "it was in front of the windows at some point. I know it was!" "No, honey," she replied with assurance, it was never there."

My sister's smug satisfaction was *not* a problem. The total outright negation of my favorite, most cherished memory devastated my spirit, and ravaged my soul. My mother's word couldn't be doubted. Had I made this up?...and fed my ego a fantasy all this time?...I can almost not express to you what thorough emptiness and despair my heart was experiencing. Were all my other recollections faulty too?... Was I a fake?... I couldn't let myself believe that, but what *could* I believe now?... Gloom entered and settled in. I felt shattered, completely bewildered, and utterly miserable.

At dinner that night, after passing the gravy to my dad, my mom said casually, "Getting back to the sofa by the way, I remember we did try it in front of the windows for a couple of days, but we didn't like it there at all."

Thank You from the bottom of my heart for that restitution, Your truth that set me free.

BAPTISM IN THE JORDAN

I dreamt one night when I was a little girl that Jesus, in a dazzling white robe, was being baptized by John the Baptist. I knew John the Baptist better than some of the other biblical characters because I belonged to his church, a beautiful big cathedral-like structure across the street from my school. But, before I go on....

I always felt very close to and comfortable with Jesus; much more so than with Mary. She strained my believing. A real live girl with no peccadillos ever? Couldn't be! And besides, she'd surely not like me either. I actually enjoyed being naughty and pesky, and sometimes went out of my way to make trouble, just for the fun of it! Jesus was different. I'd felt a kinship with Him right from the start. First of all, we had the same initials, J.C., and besides that, He died in the same state I was born in. It said so, right on the cross: INRI. In Rhode Island. So He and I were already intertwined somehow, and because I was more of a tomboy than a girl, it was much more natural to take to Him than to Mary.

Anyway, at the baptism in my dream, Jesus's feet were shin-deep in the cold running water, His robe just an inch above the rippling surface. He and John were both smiling.

Nothing too odd about this dream, but it came again the following night, exactly the same, except that this time, the cold river was chilling *my* legs...the handful of water that John scooped up and poured over Jesus trickled through *my* hair and down *my* cheeks. I was tall, bearded, and garbed in shimmering white fabric. In fact, I *was* Jesus. He and I were the same person. John had baptized *me* to the same savior mission.

At a much later date I recognized that on the left side of our church, if you face the altar, John the Baptist was immortalized in a brilliant stained-glass window, baptizing the Christ, standing shin-deep in the Jordan. What *was* there about those windows anyway, that they seemed to have had such an impact on my young soul?

FLYING HIGH

It was 1946. I was 16, a freshman at Regis College, in Weston, Massachusetts, and the world was wide and wonderful!

A small group of us were sitting under a tree on that lovely campus when a plane flew into sight. For some reason (who knows what prods us to do things?) I jumped up, ran to the open lawn in front of us, and waved hello to that beautiful silver bird and whoever was piloting him. "Get back here, you ninny," someone said. "Do you think he's going to notice you?" "I don't care," I replied, still waving my arms and smiling at the sky, "he'll know I noticed him."

As we were looking on, that beautiful silver bird, high above us, tipped his right wing low to me, and then his left, in unmistakable response to my greeting! My spirit soared up to him on wings of its own!

I still pray for that pilot now and again, when he comes to mind. I think he helped me become a believer.

A GOOD LESSON

When I heard this story for the first time, I was 18 years old. Back in 1929, the very day that ushered in the Great Depression, (which also happened to be my birthday) my dad had come home with the calamitous news that his Good Housekeeping Shops (both of them appliance stores, and very successful up to that point) had come to the end of the road. Because of the economic crash and the serious loss of income to so many families, the bank had just notified him that they had to cancel the line of credit he had relied on to run his business.

This wasn't good news, by any means, but he was trying to convince my mom that they weren't in trouble, that he was confident he'd find work, somewhere, somehow. My mom didn't panic, either. She left him for a minute and on her return, she gave him a small black bank book. Puzzled, he opened it to discover she had four thousand dollars in savings. "Where did you get all this?" he asked in amazement. "Oh, honey," she replied, "you often give me money for a new dress or a new hat...and...I want to be sure the kids can go to college..." Well, that was, in fact, the collateral needed to keep his business flourishing while so many others were losing ground and disappearing outright. I remember being dumbstruck that the intensity of her desire that we would all go to college is what fueled her frugality. Her saving, literally, helped determine our future.

What a powerful life-altering impression that made on me! In place of a more cutting-edge wardrobe, my mom had chosen to invest in our education. Wisdom, at its best, is how I saw that, and I saw it clearly. Throughout my life, this was of enormous benefit to me. For one thing, necessity is the mother of invention, so if your first thought isn't always "just buy it" you can often find or make a suitable substitution for whatever you need. That increases your creativity in all kinds of ways. My dad's philosophy helped a lot as well. "It's not what you spend," he'd say, "it's what you get for your money!"

Learning to spend wisely, and recognizing the value of such a lesson, was a gift I appreciated, and made much use of, all my life. Thanks, Mom and Dad!

MAN OF MY DREAM

Dreams were more significant in my early life than I had realized.

One night, in my late teens, I dreamt that I had been blind-folded, and had to go choose my husband from a line-up of eight men who were also blind-folded. (Never *was* able to figure that out! Why could *they* not see?)

Happily, the man I picked was George, whom I was dating among others, at the time. A sure sign, as I saw it, that God had selected him for me. That was of immense benefit to me at the moment. The fact is, (my sister Toots and I often discussed this) the message we had received repeatedly in our all-girl high-school was to never trust your feelings, nor your heart when it came to making important choices. Your mind, your reasoning should make all decisions. Never trust your feelings! Not really such good advice. (I learned this experientially once, but that's a tale of its own, later.)

Anyway, getting back to my story, the fact that George was also God's choice was truly a great comfort to me along the way, especially when the occasional but inevitable spousal conflicts surfaced. Instead of flagellating myself for having made such a hapless choice of a husband, (and I know I would have done that!) I could blame God instead…and I did, often! He had picked him out, too! That realization was always a game-changer of course, and of itself, mitigated my outrage considerably. I soon came to recognize what a singular gift that dream had been for both of us. It certainly was of much practical and valuable service to me throughout my life!

It was among the funny little treasures You blessed me with, and I cherish them all.

LIVING ROOM DRAPES

It's astounding how good You are to me! I'm really sorry I wasn't more aware of it until I got much older.

Home furnishings and decorating are not my cup of tea. To be totally honest, I think I've always been a bit fearful of not having "good taste." How silly is that? If it's *my* choice, and I like it, and my husband does too, what difference does it make if no one else does? Ah, but I was much younger then, and not very wise, I will concede.

We had just moved into our new home, and I had to pick out fabric for drapes, an agonizing task for me. After looking at too many samples, I settled on an aqua weave, and the lady left. (She had no advice for me, but, in truth, I think she wasn't a decorator, just a salesperson.) *Only* after she was gone, did I consider all the facts I should have thought about beforehand—the sectionals were plain, so was the sofa, and the carpet, too! What *on earth* made me pick out plain drapes? That was so stupid! It would be such a boring ensemble! That night, I was filled with acrid regret, and self-loathing, and set about beating my inner self to shreds. There was no way out. I couldn't face the thought of canceling my order, because it had taken the whole afternoon to make a decision, and I wasn't sure that I would make a better one the next time around. A crushing realization! I cried myself to sleep, wishing I weren't such an idiot. It was the first thing I thought of on awakening the next morning. The first thing I felt, I should say. (It's surprising how much a heavy heart can weigh!) But there was work to be done, and that can be a saving grace, sometimes.

Mid-morning, the phone rang. The saleslady from the drapery department was beside herself with all kinds of apologies. The fabric I had selected was no longer available, it should never have been among her offerings, and she was so sorry to have to disappoint me. She was coming back that very afternoon with other selections. I couldn't very well say no, but I prayed for Your help. (Come to think of it, I don't know a better decorator than You! Why didn't I think of You first?)

Long story short, the first sample I saw that day, a lovely weave of striped green, gold, and a tawny shade was the perfect choice. Took under six minutes to decide.

My favorite drapes ever! Thank You so much for discontinuing that other fabric! The perfect solution. I am *so* grateful.

A TIMELESS CONVERSATION

He was a sweet-looking little three-year-old with big expressive eyes. We were together in the den while his sister, Paulette, was napping in her bassinette in another room. I was returning an old missal to the bookshelf when a picture of Jesus—the famous Ecce Homo, (Christ's head pierced by the crown of thorns)—fell out. He picked it up immediately and seemed to be stricken by the woeful image.

It was the season of Lent and in answer to his questions I started to toddler-talk to him about the troubles Jesus was having at that time. He thirsted for stories constantly. I got the children's Bible for illustrations and we sat on the sofa together. His eyes and ears drank in every detail and suddenly, with tears in his voice, he blurted out: "Why didn't Blessed Mother yell "Stop it! Stop that, you bad men!" His passion arrested me, and made me realize that so often, (maybe most of the time) Jesus-stories are not clearly *real* to our minds. His reaction made me see that account in a much fresher dimension myself, that morning.

Paulette's crying interrupted our conversation. He turned to me, brown eyes brimming with concern, and asked, "Is he feeling better, now, Mom?"... which locked this humble little incident in my heart forever.

A VISION - May 26, 1955

(This piece is exactly what I wrote down, word for word, 64 years ago, after having fallen asleep, once Valerie was born. Not simple to read or understand, guaranteed!)

"George delivered our third child, Valerie, early this morning at about 4:00 AM by himself, at home. I have to put this down *immediately* and preserve a fragment of the great and wondrous dream I had after her birth. Maybe it was an omen, a prophecy, or an oracle of sorts, or maybe it was just the product of my usually active imagination that hadn't had enough stimulus of late.

This dream—this vision—was so tremendous in scope! In it I learned that of, say, a million years or some such fantastic stretch of time, only one individual was needed to have that age interpreted by the real masterminds of human culture—people living some hundred thousand years hence. Each epoch was like a letter, forming a word, but working backwards. The message would be completed only at the end of time. The whole story of mankind, before civilization, before any history was recorded for instance, constituted the letter M. Eons later, a new period of evolution and expansion and inventive theories etc. added the letter S. This information was always provided by a single individual with a great destiny who was not given to see his or her part in this stupendous world-puzzle-word. The word was up to ISM, when through this baby of ours and her life, somehow it would be advanced to PHISM. She was the individual who would matter most for our entire modern era.

In this dream, I was a spirit, seeing all of this in fast slow-motion, and was ecstatically numb to know that something I had touched ever so slightly, someone I was related to, could be so vitally connected to the secret and mystery of the universe. Yet I knew, seeing the great overall picture of the cosmos in this way, that parent and child relationship is a mere brushing of wings…little people produce great geniuses who produce simpletons and so on, back and forth, and none of it is of any significance at all. I awoke realizing I'd been exceedingly privileged to have had even a glimpse of such ethereal workings, and believing firmly that this child must have some special destiny, whatever it be. A veiled and mysterious feeling…

Only later today did I learn that she had been born 'a caul baby,' wholly encapsulated in a membrane from which George had to extricate her after delivery. (Old wives' tales always attributed special gifts and powers to these children.) Had I known of the caul, I would easily have dismissed this dream as an imaginative by-product of that information. I thank God I knew nothing about it. "

IN GOD'S TIME

Our infant daughter, Sylvia, had gotten her first vaccination that afternoon, and we were getting home later than I had anticipated. Once settled, I opened a new bottle of baby aspirin and removed one tiny orange tablet to crush into applesauce for her. I set the container way back on the counter under a shelf. She was wailing uncomfortably and I was eager to give her a little relief. After putting her in her crib, I went down to the game room to transfer clothes from the washer to the dryer, before getting dinner ready.

Later that evening, after the kids (Charl, 5, Paulette, 4, and Valerie, 2) were in bed, I was down there folding clothes, when in a sudden shock, I remembered the aspirin, still on the counter. I ran frantically up the stairs and as I got to the kitchen, George was calling down to me from the second floor that Paulette was vomiting. I dashed to the counter first, praying my suspicions weren't valid. When the bottle wasn't there, I ran to the wastebasket in the closet. Sure enough, a totally empty little bottle! I jumped on the phone, and Dr. Dashef, our pediatrician, agreed to meet us at the hospital immediately.

When the pumping procedure was over, they told us, had we been twenty minutes later, it would have been too late.

How could I e-v-e-r have forgiven myself that carelessness? I can't even bear to think about it... Lord, thank you so much for Paulette's life, and for having spared me that ever-lasting torment.

MARGE and BOB

My friend Marge was behind me as we made our way slowly down the aisle to receive Communion.   Bob, a sweet young adult in our parish, who was more than moderately compromised mentally, was sitting in the front pew which we were approaching.

Marge told me later that it had suddenly come to her with goosebumps, that he was the individual closest to God in our entire congregation.   "I will reach out and touch his sleeve," she said to herself, "and I, too, will be filled with Godliness."

"But," she continued, "when you approached, he reached up and touched *your* sleeve! You smiled at him, and covered his hand with your own, gently, eliciting an adoring smile in return…and in witnessing that exchange" she said, "I felt God enter me, as well."

MEET ALICE

Meet Alice. She saved my life. At least, she saved me from growing into a grisly grouch, resentful of my labor-laden life and all its duties. This was eons ago, of course, when I was a young mother with six kids under nine. Granted, there was lots to do, but it was actually a misunderstanding of my Christian tradition that was doing me in.

Growing up as a child, my siblings and I (all in Catholic schools, and of wonderful parents with sound values) were other-oriented from the word go. (How blessed we were!) Love your neighbor we learned early. God was good to us, we'd be good to everybody. It made perfect sense, so we never gave it a second thought. Going the extra mile was a way of life, and my choice, really, but after nine years of babies and diapers, and toddlers and school kids and homework and lunches and scrubbing and carting, and laundry, I was LOSING IT!... because I was losing me, and didn't realize it.

Maybe some women could go on giving, never counting the cost, but we also grew up with total fairness in our genes, thankfully. I never could shout aloud, "Look at me! I can't keep this up! I need a day off!" because that smacked of selfishness. (This was my job, wasn't it? Then stop moaning, and get it done!) There were many gripes and much complaining in my mind and heart. Truth be told, I could hear nothing else.

One day (thank you, Lord!) it occurred to me to call myself not Mom, not Jackie, but Alice. I lined us all up (in my head) and thought: "Oh my gosh, look at Alice! LOOK AT ALICE!! She needs HELP!" I never could have screamed that for myself, but it was a natural reaction to what was there. It was FAIR and way overdue! There was no selfishness involved, only a clear-sighted and rightful determination to help that poor woman, Alice, who was definitely on overload, and had been, for some time. It was a joy and a relief to reapportion chores to everyone. Halleluiah!

I credit Alice with teaching me to include ME, when I was being fair to everyone. (Take a good look. "Love your neighbor"… ends with…"as yourself!")

THE SPIRIT and the ABBEY

It was March of 1960, early afternoon. I was in the den nursing Helene, our latest addition to the family, when my Aunt Aurore came by to meet our new baby. As she bent over us, the pendant on her neck-chain, a silver dove, swung to and fro in slow easy motion…to and fro…to and fro…back and forth. It seemed, somehow, to be begging for my attention. When I recognized it as the Holy Spirit, I realized with a little pang that, other than at Confirmation, He had never been a component of my life at all, and I needed Him! I needed His gifts. In a flash, my whole inner being was on fire!…burning!…to apologize profusely for having ignored Him for so long…to invite Him to take over my life…to beg His help in bringing our children up well…to guide me in striving for…WHOA!!-WHOA.!!! I felt I was reining in a run-away horse!! It jolted me, actually, that my spirit had taken such complete control of my senses for a minute, there, (though I will sheepishly confess that I am occasionally swept away like that, especially if it involves other-worldliness,) but this overly energetic reaction did flabbergast me. I was back to normal (thank goodness) before Aunt Aurore stopped cooing at the baby, and turned to me.

During dinner that evening, George was telling us of a phone call he'd received that day at the office. Sister Gertrude was calling from Mt. St. Mary's Abbey, a monastery in nearby Wrentham, Massachusetts. Their dentist had just retired and she was asking George if he would consider replacing him and come to the abbey once a month. "We can only offer you prayers and chocolate," she said, adding that he could think it over for two weeks before responding. (Making and marketing delicious chocolate confections supplies the abbey's income.) "Thank you, Sister," was his reply. "I don't need two weeks. I'll say 'yes' right now." Thus began for our family a lovely, life-long, heartwarming relationship with the Cistercian (Trappistine) nuns. A heavenly gift, indeed.

In no time, Dr. George modernized their existing clinic with equipment contributed from various dental supply houses. With the nuns' permission, he invited three other dentists to participate, each donating one day a month. Two of the Sisters became dental assistants twice a month. The whole community was most appreciative of the professional prowess from which they were soon benefitting. Given the location of their abbey in MA, however, and the fact that George and his confreres practiced in RI, we often wondered how he had come to be selected, initially. When Sr. Gertrude was a patient one day, he questioned her about it. "We didn't have a clue," she said, "We all prayed together to the Holy Spirit that afternoon for a good dentist, drew a pencil down the yellow pages, and stopped where He told us to."

George reveled in his years of service to them, and how could he not have? Fifty of the world's sweetest and most beautiful women loved and prayed for him daily, offering him almond bark to boot! An admittedly bountiful blessing. Our son, Joel, is now their dentist, and is happy to offer them the same level of dental perfection that was his father's trademark. Before he left this world, George happily voiced several times, what a comfort it was to him that his much-loved Sisters would continue to have truly excellent care through the next generation.

The first paragraph of this story, you may have realized, is totally irrelevant to the rest of the tale. What's it doing there? It actually wasn't there, originally. It wasn't until months later that I made the connection myself, and it intrigued me intensely. That same day, (the very same afternoon, mind you!) that all the nuns were fervently beseeching the Holy Spirit to find them a good dentist, I was pleading with Him myself, in the den, (and *really* into it, remember?) My spirit was *imploring* Him to become a more vital part of my life. Can you believe He was tuned in to both of us, begging for favors at the exact same time...and then, flooded our lives with His fulfillment! I found that correlation exciting. I liked that it linked me somehow, even ever so slightly, to that memorable monastery call out of the blue!

Thank You, up there!

The KOOL-AID STORY

There were about ten neighborhood children, all under the age of ten, having a great time at the front of our house, jumping off the brick steps at different heights and then boosting their skills trying out the next level. Their joyful shrieks proclaimed the thrill of success, over and over. I was thoroughly enjoying their play, which I could hear clearly from the kitchen.

It suddenly occurred to me to invite them all in for Kool-Aid. (Say again?? What mom, in her right mind, would invite a bunch of kids *in*, when the only move to be considered was—*incontrovertibly*—to take a pitcher and plastic cups *out there*!) Sticky spills and messy dribbles are much better on the grass, than on my vinyl floor, for sure! I knew that. I knew that very well. Yet, totally against my better judgment, (why was I doing this?...) I rounded them up, and ushered all of them into the house.

As soon as the last one had crossed the threshold into the kitchen, we heard and felt an ominous thundering! The whole house seemed to shake on its foundation for a minute! Was this an earthquake?? I ran to the window in the den, to see if our neighbors' home across the street was intact, and my blood congealed at what I saw! The Allens' big black Oldsmobile had rolled backwards, and crashed dead center into the brick steps in our front yard. Its brakes must have just let go, and the momentum the car picked up, rolling down the incline of their driveway, propelled it forcefully and directly to our front steps, where seconds earlier, ten happy children had been at play.

Battered fenders and broken bricks…but thanks to Your nod, Lord, not battered bodies and broken hearts.

You are my Savior, and theirs.

IPM

There'd been a short blurb in our local newspaper that IPM, the Inner Peace Movement, was going to be introduced to the general public at a meeting on Wednesday evening at 7:30 PM at the Woonsocket Motor Inn. In addition to helping people find inner peace, there would be a discussion of ESP, Extra-Sensory-Perception, the gifted power that everyone has, of which very few ever make use. I was much interested in the former and absolutely hooked when I read about the latter. How fascinating! I couldn't wait to be there.

It occurred to me to wonder though, if this new venture that held such appeal for me would, in fact, bring me closer to God, or possibly alienate me from Him in any way, however slight. A question to ponder, for sure, before any novel undertaking, but I've come to believe that I'm free to follow all roads if I just hold on to His hand. Anyway, going to bed that night I mentioned my concern to Him. I didn't get any indication that He wanted me to stay away...good! After my prayers, I drifted off immediately, as I always do. (A favorite, much appreciated blessing, thank You!)

When Wednesday came around, I had completely forgotten about the meeting. (How COULD I have???) I was ironing in the evening at about 7:00 PM when a friend called. "Oh," she said, "I'm surprised you're home. I almost just hung up because I was sure you'd be at that IPM meeting." I knew immediately that God was reaching out to remind me because He knew I wanted to be there! I thanked her for calling, told her I'd get back to her in the morning, and scooted.

Thank You AGAIN, Lord, for not letting me miss it! YOU were at all those meetings!

24

CAMPING TRIP

My sister Muriel and her family were campers, and went off frequently in their cozy little—but oh, so functional—trailer, to various campgrounds, and out-of-the-way places. That seemed to be life at its simplest and most basic level, and was so appealing to me!

Several years later, when the youngest of our six children was four, and mobility as a family was a little more manageable, we became interested in the possibility of a camping vacation. (I say "we", but the fact is, we, the kids and I, were interested. Their father was not. It took our combined pleas, prayers and persuasive powers to convince him that he might enjoy it too…and good sport that he was, he finally agreed.)

We had the week of the 4th of July. Bright and early that Saturday morning, we arrived at the Silver Lake camping site in New Hampshire, a little surprised that we were the only ones there. My sister had told me that reservations couldn't be made ahead. It was always first come, first served. As we approached the kiosk and inquired about a location, the lady there smiled at me supremely sarcastically, and said in the same tone: "Oh, you're here to camp, are you? Did you expect to just drive in?" My look of shocked disbelief must have fueled her fancy. "I turned away 134 cars yesterday" she continued, "but you were going to fool us and come today, right?" Her smug complacency seared my nerve endings, but she was right. I actually *was* as brainless as she was imagining! No thought of Plan B had ever entered my mind. A little unnerved at this development, we pulled into a parking space at a complete loss of where to go or what to do next. A sign on a nearby tree indicated the path to the lake. "I'll take the kids to the water for a minute to unwind," I said to George. "Think about what we're going to do, and so will I," …and frantically, I fought the thought of the trailer sitting in our driveway all week!

Still in desperation on our way back from the lake, we passed a lovely tree-shaded site where a couple was working on a pop-up-trailer. Having heard many times from my sister how friendly campers always are, I asked if we could watch the procedure.

They welcomed our attention whole-heartedly and asked if we were staying there. As I briefly explained our predicament, to my utter amazement, the woman we were speaking with smiled broadly and said, "Listen, it's supposed to rain all day tomorrow, that's why we're going home today, but because it's still ours, we can actually transfer it to you right now. C'mon, let's go to the kiosk." In deliriously delightful disbelief, we followed her to the booth. "Monica," she said, "Bob and I are leaving this afternoon. We want to give our spot to this lady and her family." To my astonishment, Monica's expression soured visibly before our eyes! She turned an angry face to me and snorted: "You must have been born with a silver spoon in your mouth!"

I remember that I felt sorry for her that she could be so annoyed by someone else's good fortune, rather than rejoice with them! But *rejoice, we did*...and *we thanked God earnestly,* that He was so loving and giving!

A rich and rewarding week. Sometimes still my heart breaks into song over it, so grateful am I, even to this day, for the memory of that sweet little miracle just for us!

TWO DAYS

I haven't thought about this occurrence in a very long time, yet it was one of the most divining moments of my life, an almost unbelievably powerful experience, and I am so grateful for it. How could I ever have let myself forget it, even for an instant? Let it fade like this? I hope and trust that only my consciousness can lose sight of these events occasionally—that they are eternally engraved in the substance of my soul. One great benefit to me, of writing these incidents down, is to crystallize them forever and have instant and detailed recall at will. Our mortal minds and memories fade with age and I don't want to lose any of this, ever, or exaggerate it in memory, either.

It was shortly after Christmas, 1964. Our Mexican exchange student who'd been with us for a month had just left. Did it have anything to do with him? I used to think it came from having agreed to take him in, not a very convenient time after all, because I always overdid during the holidays. But then the realization came to me that Christmas is the very best time to welcome anyone into your home, particularly a stranger. That did it. His name was Emilio and we all loved him!

I awoke one morning a few days after he was gone and *knew*, immediately, that I was in another zone. A zone of *pure love*. That's what I was breathing in and exhaling. I remember bending over to tie my shoe and it was an action motivated by, and accomplished, in perfect love. Tying my shoe was momentous, was a kind of tribute to the Creator—an acknowledgement that all things rightfully begin and live and end in love. Every thought and every movement during the whole day was the same. I was in the presence of Love, in the kingdom of Love. I was a being of total Love, myself.

All creation sang in praise. Every branch of every tree sounded a special note. I heard them. Rocks had a hum of their own. Icicles, clouds, clumps of earth and fields fluted gloriously in honor and adoration. Tears added their tinkling. It was the most inexpressibly magnificent blend of sound, and it reverberated love and gratitude and praise and joy…and I could understand it clearly. I was a part of this glorious cheering, and it lasted all day.

When I went to bed that night, so grateful for this unimaginably wondrous experience, I tried to fill my being with that heavenly music, knowing that it was a once-in-a-lifetime privilege. Still, it had been a "normal" day —laundry, meals, cleaning, kids' quarrels, etc.— I was fully into what I was doing, yet I was deep, deep into the most profound love of all things. You.

In the morning I awoke and, incredibly, I was still there, still in that blissful realm for another entire day. I was part of that symphony again, that melody of the spheres that resonates recognition and reverence and exaltation. I myself was holy, and wholly Love…one day more.

Thank you. I so delighted in, and appreciate Your having let me resound your praise with all of creation.

A LITTLE CHILD SHALL LEAD THEM

Joel was four years old. He came in from outdoors one day and asked me, "Mom, can a house give glory to God?" My spirit *thrilled* at his interest. ("Take this further," my mind said to me, "you want to teach him that a man can think, and that's what makes all the difference!") "Yes, of course, Joel," I replied, "but what would you say gives Him more glory," I continued, "a house or a man?"

He looked at me as if I had two heads…and laughed. "A man, of course," he chortled. "Why, honey?" I persisted. He smiled. "Mom, you know why…because a house can't love!"

Thank You that he stopped me dead in my tracks, with the right answer!

DAMP SHEETS

Helene was ten years old. I had asked her to take in the sheets from the clothesline, which she did. When I got to them downstairs in the game-room where she had left them, I realized they were still damp, much too damp to have been removed from the line. I would have to hang them out again. Wouldn't you think someone ten years old would have enough sense to know that sheets had to be dry before you took them in? What was she thinking?

I fumed my way up the stairs ready to lay her out in lavender for being so clueless. She deserved it. I was really annoyed. However, in the middle of climbing those stairs an astonishing thing happened, and I'm so glad and grateful it did. It came to me that those same sheets had been folded beautifully, nice even corners, perfectly flat squares, no bunching inside at all. She happened to step into the hall as I got up there. "Helene, what great work you did folding those sheets," I said, " I've never seen a better job. They were perfect!" As I spoke, I was realizing that I didn't often overdo the compliments. (I usually expect things to be done right, that's the policy here. If they're not, I will bring it up, but done right is the way it should be, and that's that.) I added, more gently than usual for some reason, "but, honey, if they're still damp, you have to let them dry on the line before you take them in."

Her reaction reinforced my gnawing suspicion that I rarely commended my children. "Mom," she asked, her eyes glowing with pleasure, "is that really true? Did I really do the best job you ever saw?" and the light beaming from her face, the pride in her smile and the satisfaction with herself that she was obviously relishing, left me speechless, and stopped my heart too. *THIS* was how you corrected children!! Here I was, understanding the technique for the first time…and our fifth child was ten years old! She ran off to play, and I went to our bedroom, crying burning tears for the years I had messed up, but deeply appreciating Your grace and wisdom, so newly recognized.

MILLINOCKET BEAR

My two sisters and I, with a few friends, were on a white-water rafting trip in Maine. While having dinner in the lodge the night before our trek on the Penobscot River, I asked our friendly waiter what their guests did for entertainment on a Saturday evening. "Lots of 'em go to the dump to watch the bears," he said. "Not much else to do around here." Sounded like fun to us.

As we were leaving the lodge, I stuck my head in the kitchen and asked for scraps that might help lure the bears and left with a bagful. It was a five-mile drive to the dump, and a five-dollar admission fee. There were already several cars parked there. Right off, we could see a black bear about the length of a football field away. "Listen," I said to my friends, "sometimes I can be a little foolhardy but I don't think it would be reckless behavior to just step out a little and throw some food in his direction, do you?...to attract him a bit closer?" They were all in favor.

I walked about eight feet past the car and immediately tossed bread, bones, and a few chunks of cake. As I did this, the passenger in the nearest car rolled down his window and whispered hoarsely to me, "Don't look now, lady, but there's a bear right beside you." My blood turned to ice in my veins because I had just noticed him myself! He was about my size, black and furry, and just a few feet away! My whole body seemed to turn into mush. My legs felt like two dishrags, hardly able to hold me up...and just barely, with my face eyeing the ground only, could I move each one backward, deliberately...one at a time...but slowly and shakily. "Oh Lord, what was I doing in their territory?"

What the bear's reaction was, I have no idea. My feeble legs *did* manage to retreat to the rear door of the car which my friends opened, and in grateful anguish, I collapsed on the back seat.

Today, and every day of my life, I thank You for Your help!

ORDER

I was shaking bed sheets outside an upstairs window. My mind was working overtime, because the whole house was in disarray, and I was mentally prioritizing all the tasks before me. "I hate to have everything so messed up," I thought. "I love order." I had never articulated that so specifically before, and, for some reason it arrested my attention. I had always thought of myself as spontaneous and effervescent…but I realized I was changing my allegiance, so to speak. As if to validate my new creed, I said aloud to the sky, with my head out the window, "I love order!" I looked up at God and said one more time, insistently, "I have a *passion* for *order!*"

So? What's the big deal here? Why would I even remember this?

That very same night, I went to the Inner Peace Meeting, (IPM) for the first time. The moderator explained to us that most people operated out of one of four categories. They were either visionary; feeler; intuitive; or prophet. "Prophets," he described, "have a little of each category, but mainly, they have a passion for order."

Just like that, I knew where I belonged. Thanks!

WITH MINOU'S HELP

It was Sunday. The Gospel was being read to us in church. "Unless you eat My Flesh and drink My Blood, you will not have eternal life within you"...and according to Scripture, at those words, half the crowd left. "I'm not surprised, Lord," I said. "I would have left, too. We just don't do that. We don't eat each other! What on earth could You have been thinking of?" I felt bad railing against Him like that, but it's really crucial to not fake your believing, even to yourself.

Driving home, though, I thought more about it. "Listen, Lord," I said, "I'm positive that every line in your Bible is right and works for our benefit. I'm just not understanding it properly, so please, help me see that the way You do."

I'd think about it every now and then, but a week or so later, when I was in the kitchen, Helene's pregnant cat, Minou, came to her feeding dish. (Truth be told, I wasn't terribly fond of her, but Helene loved her dearly, and that was enough.) As I looked at her swollen body, it came to me that those kitten embryos were being nourished by cat flesh and blood...and that's what would make them cats, of course. Every living mammal *has* to be nourished for a period of time, on its parent's flesh and blood, to turn into whatever was nourishing it—cats—cows—kids, and all of a sudden, my mind exploded! I realized that Jesus left us His Body and Blood in the Eucharist for just that reason. As He was telling the crowd, *we have to be nourished by that Body and Blood*, while we're here, to become Divinity ourselves! We are all in a gestation period on this earth, preparing for another kind of life.

33

Humanity is God's masterpiece, and the only species that can actually choose its destination, thanks to free will. We can live here, totally ignoring our divine origin and not seeking to develop it in any way, or we can respond to God's multiple overtures, and help ourselves progress into Divinity—the destiny available to us, *if we choose* to be nourished by God's own Body and Blood, which He left here for just that purpose! WOW!

Minou, thank you for being so instrumental in helping me *see* the unimaginably awesome truth of what Jesus was telling us! How can I not appreciate and love you more, now?

THE STILL SMALL VOICE

This was in response to the IPM (Inner Peace Movement) suggestion to get into the habit of recognizing that still, small voice within.

I was soon to be meeting my sister, Toots, for lunch. At the moment, I was making a sauce in the kitchen. I thought I heard that still small voice telling me to call Toots and let her know that if I didn't get there, she should come here to my house. (That was weird. I had every intention of being there, why would I send a message like that and confuse her? Then again, why would I get a message like that for nothing? And isn't learning to trust that little voice what this was all about?) I called her and laughingly gave her the memo, explaining that I was definitely planning to go, but that I was responding to the still, small voice within that I wanted to get to know better. She understood me completely.

I finished the sauce, got the baby dressed, and carried her out to the car. As I was putting her in the car seat, the unmistakable odor that assailed me and necessitated a trip back into the house for a quick diaper change made me chuckle. I certainly would never abandon my plans just because of this. I'd be late, that's all. Is this insignificance what that little voice was warning me about? That surprised me. I finished what had to be done and hurried out. It was later than I thought.

As I was closing the breezeway door, with the baby in my arms, she reached out and in a flash, had slid four tiny fingers directly into the crack as I pulled hard and shut the door tight.

Trust me. You can trust that still, small voice.

A WHOLE FAMILY OF CATS

Aunt Aurore had given my siblings and me a calendar for Christmas that year. A spiritual thought for each day was printed on the bottom under the date. But here's some background for my story: Helene's cat, Minou, had just had six kittens. None of our friends were interested in adopting. (Not even with dowries!) The pet shop didn't want them, and I was not interested in drowning live kittens. A distressing dilemma.

On this particular morning, the thought for the day read: "There is nothing so insignificant in your life that the Holy Spirit isn't interested." "Oh yeah?" I retorted, (out loud, mind you, and a little less than politely, too, considering that I might be speaking to God!) "Well then, You just find me someone for my whole family of cats, and I might believe it!" A short while later, an old college friend stopped by to tell me she had recently moved. She was still in Cumberland but in a more rural area. There was a barn on her new property. When Minou came into view with all her babies trailing her, Ann looked directly at me and said: "That's just what I need right now, a whole family of cats." I leaped from my chair in my exuberance! That was less than three quarters of an hour after I had so boldly challenged the Holy Spirit. And He answered with my very own words! How awesome was that?

What an exciting moment…to have been responded to so personally, by God Himself! My soul has been doing cartwheels since that encounter. (Though I will admit to feeling a bit embarrassed by my sassy response through the calendar. Not a bit nice, but I *have* apologized.)

Honestly, I can hardly believe it!! The Master of the universe and all the galaxies knows *who I am*…and heard, and solved my most pressing problem. Halleluiah!

THIS MAN IS YOU

One day, I was sitting in the downstairs bathroom, facing the wall. The sunlight coming from the window on my right reflected my head and neck on the opposite wall in the strangest, most compelling way. It was absolutely fascinating…dark shadows and light ones, deep hollows, and eerie, irregular patches suggested a face and features, but nothing definite was discernible. It was my reflection, however, archetypically human…not male, nor female, neither young nor old. It seemed to be seeing from its black depth eye sockets, but it was, and seemed eternally meant to be, silent. Stone still and silent.

I was riveted to the sight. Light and shadow had affixed me to the surface of the wall and let me see my soul in Rorschach. The essence of me was what it was looking at and what it was showing me, simultaneously. I was truly mesmerized…and mute, like my mentor on the wall. "This is you," I finally said aloud to myself, slowly and deliberately, after long minutes of musing. "This shadowy specter symbol that will disappear as soon as you stand is a truer likeness of you than anything you've ever seen. You are, at the core of you, that formless faceless force projected to the wall, and yet, not there. Who are you, anyway?" I asked it, distinctly. "What are you showing me?"

Melodramatic dalliance, I agree, but it had an impact of sorts.

The next day, Father Brown, our Christian Family Movement moderator stopped by. "I came to bring you this book." he said. "I thought you'd find it interesting." He handed it to me, backside-to. I thanked him and turned it to see the cover. There, under the black print title, THIS MAN IS YOU, my half-formed, hollow-eyed, *identical* self-portrait of yesterday looked deep again into my soul.

A CLOSE CALL

Charlie, paddling solo in the canoe, pulled up to me at the lake, and said, "Hop in, Mom, I just spotted a great raspberry patch not too far from here." We were relative newcomers to Lake Arrowhead in Maine, and ample native blueberries and raspberries were part of the fun. I should have gone back for my clogs, but I didn't. I hopped right out of the water into the canoe. A short while later, we arrived at a section of land that I wasn't at all familiar with, but I love exploring, so that was no problem. The problem *was*, however, that the ground there was so prickly, pebbly, and sharp to my bare feet, that I could hardly take three steps without seriously painful discomfort. I stayed where I was, and Charl followed the path around the bend to fruitfulness.

It was such a treat to be here, our first summer in the woods of Maine, in a sweet little cottage just a step or two above a shack, but so cozy and cute. Nothing artificial or commercial for miles around! A heavenly spot, and I was enjoying every minute of it no matter where I was. Suddenly, the noise of something at a distance, rustling in the brush, disturbed my reverie. Some animal, rather large, judging from the sound it made, was approaching rapidly. Then I saw them. Two big dogs foaming at the mouth, but with teeth visibly gleaming, were heading hell-bent for me! My very first thought was that they would make ground beef of me in jig time—and that's what Charl would find when he came back. Instantaneously, though, I remembered having read somewhere that the human scent of fear is what engenders and intensifies an animal's ferocity, so I immediately set my will consciously to produce an odor from my skin, a courageous "I'm not afraid of you!" smell. I forcefully exuded it from my pores. I could almost detect it myself, so intent was I on creating this odoriferous life-saving shield...and all of this in a nano-second, not more!

The dogs literally lunged at me with gaping jaws, their slobbering jowls at my bare thighs for an excruciating eternity of seconds. I stood firm and resolute, with clenched fists, swelling my "you don't scare me" smell to the high heavens...from whence came my salvation! Both dogs sniffed forcefully at my groin once or twice more, almost knocking me over, and then abruptly, together, turned and trotted down to the water's edge.

The ordeal was over, just like that...and heaven and I had beaten them at their own game! Thanks, Lord.

PENTECOST SUNDAY

One Friday evening, I was sitting by myself in a lecture hall that was rapidly filling up. (I'm seldom early for anything, but that night for some reason, I had arrived a full fifteen minutes ahead of time.) I happened to look up as a gentleman opened the door and entered.

To my utter astonishment, my entire inner being responded to his appearance with surprisingly intense gratitude flooding my soul. Never before had I experienced such a clear, conscious, recognition of anything, in my whole life! My spirit was *swelling* with crystal-clear appreciation and gratefulness...and I had no clue whatsoever to this man's identity. What a mystifying and fascinating situation to be in! For me, there was absolutely no denying some kind of heartfelt connection between us.

I was so intrigued that I planned to join him immediately wherever he sat. He came directly to the empty chair beside me. I recounted to him everything I just told you. We had never met. "Are you a writer?" I asked. "Maybe I read something of yours that resonated with me." He was not a writer. "What do you do?" I asked him point-blank. "I'm a Greymoor Friar," he replied.

(Their monastery of past years is now part of our local library. Occasionally back then, a Greymoor priest would say Mass at St. Aidan's, located very nearby. I had attended Mass there for the first time a few months before, on Pentecost Sunday. The sermon I heard that morning moved me so profoundly, that a poem welled right up from the depths of me in thanksgiving. I had written it out and left it in the pew.)

40

"Did you by any chance celebrate the 10:00 Mass at St. Aidan's on Pentecost Sunday?" I inquired, expectantly. "No," he responded, disintegrating my hope. Two moments later though, he turned to me again, and said, "I'm sorry. I'm just remembering... I did, in fact, replace a priest who was ill, at the 10:00 Mass on Pentecost Sunday."

Though I hadn't recognized him, Thank You that I *felt* Your truth.

WEEKEND IN WASHINGTON

Our daughter, Sylvia, had been selected Presidential Scholar of RI in 1975. Quite an honor. There was an official communication in our mailbox addressed to us from the White House, inviting us to Washington, D.C. for the weekend. It was all very exciting.

The first evening there we were hosted at the State Department, where royalty and heads-of-state are always entertained. An impressive reception. I had particularly enjoyed a conversation with Jean ____, assistant to Caspar Weinberger, Secretary of Health, Education and Welfare, under President Gerald Ford. The last event of the weekend was the ceremony in the Rose Garden, at 1600 Pennsylvania Avenue, where the medals and citations would be awarded by the President to the individual scholars. We, the parents, were in a long line waiting for admission to the garden.

One security officer passing by stopped abruptly and asked where my official name tag was. Inwardly confronting a sudden surge of malaise, I replied that I had packed it in my suitcase with other memorabilia from the weekend, because we were heading right back to RI after the presentations. He said, "Ma'am, you won't be allowed into the garden without identification. Does anyone here know you, other than your husband?" My heart did a sick flip — of course no one knew me. My suitcase was in the trunk of the car, back at the hotel. By the time I retrieved it, the ceremony would be over. How incredibly stupid of me to be missing a national award being presented to our daughter! I could hardly face my own imbecility without crying. Aware of my acute distress, his tone *did* become more gentle. "I'm sorry, ma'am, you'll just have to wait out here with me." Even as he spoke, the line started to move forward. I was in torment!

At that precise moment, my friend of Friday evening, Jean ____, sauntered down the street with friends. "Hi, Jackie," she called out with a smile. The officer spun around.

"Miss ____," he addressed her, "you know this woman?" "I do," she responded, "we met Friday evening at the reception. Is there a problem?" "No, ma'am," he replied. "Thank you for stopping by."

You save me over and over again! How can I not love You forever and trust You completely, when I have such constant proof of Your goodness and Your enduring patience with my utter incompetence!?

BLACK FLIES

Jossi was a little cutie, almost three years old. She had spent last summer totally enraptured with water. She'd jump into the pool if she saw you there, whether you'd seen her coming or not. At the lake, she'd walk in without hesitation, up to her neck…a very upsetting scenario, if you were her mom. This summer was totally different. She couldn't be enticed into the water at all. Not for any reason, not even for a minute. It was really peculiar, but by the end of the season we had all grown accustomed to it. So much so, that my husband and I felt confident leaving her in the pool area with her siblings in their teens. It was a private pool at the clubhouse in Maine, and this particular morning we were the only people there. She wore a little sundress, not a bathing suit, and played with her doll by the fence. The tennis courts were close by. George and I decided to have a quick game. Very poor decision.

Well into the set, I was serving when the black flies started pestering me. I'd toss the ball and let it fall as I swatted the pesky flies in my face. I did this several times. Annoyed at my behavior, George shouted to me across the court not to be such a baby, and to hit the ball. Any partner might have said the same thing, but my response was to throw down my racket, a la prima donna, and stomp off the court in a huff. The reasonable section of my mind was beside itself! (I had made great strides in past years, modifying the blaze that my anger could sometimes ignite under the slightest provocation.) I recognized this sullen departure as serious overreaction. "Don't be a fool!" I commanded myself, as I stalked out of the fenced-in area. "Get back there! You're going to undo all the progress you've been making all these years! Don't *do* this! Oh, Jackie, *go back*!" The more desperately my mind pleaded with me to return, the more determinedly I ignored its logic and marched doggedly on right straight to where the children were.

As I opened the gate to the swimming area, I saw Jossi trotting along the cement on the near side of the pool. The other kids were all at the far end by the diving board. At that very instant, she stubbed her toe, flipped up and over somehow, and landed headfirst in the burbling water, *unnoticed* by anyone but me. Exhilarated to be there at that moment when no one else had seen it happen, I dove in and rescued her instantly, overwhelmingly thankful to God for having sent those black flies to goad me to her side.

The gift of a lifetime, *again*, Lord. I am boundlessly grateful.

AUNT AURORE

A newspaper article recently stated that a child born in 1904 had a life expectancy of 47 years. It caught my eye because that was Aunt Aurore's birth year. Despite being a sickly child she beat the statistics of longevity by more than half a century! I thank God that she did, because every year as she got older she loved more. What an amazing and awesome phenomenon to observe! I pray we do as well.

At her 100th birthday party, a friend of hers who belonged to the Oblates of Mary Immaculate, as did my aunt, asked me if I would please write an article about Aunt Aurore for their magazine. (Roughly, this is it.) Well, my own personal relationship with her started shakily. My earliest remembrance of her (I was four) was that she suggested to my mother that I should wear "bangs." My mother was readily persuaded. In jig time, Aunt Aurore had cornered me and was snipping away enthusiastically, totally ignoring my scowl. (Hey, it's *my* hair! How come no one asked *my* permission?) The following week, she showed up in the kitchen with mushrooms—which we had not previously sampled—again impelling us to leave our comfort zone, in food as well as fashion. Good move, but we weren't quite ready for it.

It was through Aunt Aurore, too, that we were introduced to the culture of our heritage, by attending parties sponsored by L'Alliance Francaise where ladies spoke a language with accents unfamiliar, and little girls had to wear best dresses and behave all afternoon. Not very appealing. (How could she think we'd enjoy that?) Despite the challenges, as I grew up, my aunt seemed to me to be the quintessential career woman. She held a very responsible position at the Blackstone Valley Gas and Electric Co. She was highly thought of and respected by her superiors, and always looked stunning, dressed in the latest style. (She had even rejected romance and a marriage proposal, which intrigued me no end!)

Well, that was a young niece's simple evaluation of an aunt whose grace and wisdom perhaps eluded the youngster's comprehension. She was also an excellent pianist and a talented member of Alexander Peloquin's famous chorale. My first appreciation of her devotedness was her involvement in her home parish, Precious Blood, where every week she sang in the choir, counted and tallied budget envelopes and assisted in sundry other capacities. Her readiness to help others also led her to volunteer at Hospice St. Antoine in North Smithfield as well as at the Epheta Retreat House in Manville.

In her 50s, Aunt Aurore learned to drive a car, a feat we all applauded heartily. It was then, too, that she became an Oblate of Mary Immaculate, an equally important step, to be sure, but one that went unheralded by us, because we didn't learn about it until years later.

During her declining years Aunt Aurore was a resident at Hospice St. Antoine, where she used to volunteer. Many days when I was visiting, we held delightful and inspiring conversations, full of enlightenment. I was in awe, truly, at the depth of her understanding. Though truth be told, there *were* days when she would accuse me of having stolen her car keys, and just *wouldn't* let up! Another time, she welcomed me very formally and politely, convinced that I was a French guest speaker from the University of Montreal. No amount of reasoning or protest would dissuade her from that concept. It was perfect though, because, despite the fact that I used to ask her to speak French with me (I needed the practice) she never stayed with it very long. That afternoon, however, we never strayed from it. We spoke perfect French not missing a single "liaison" or "double negatif!" It was really more amusing than astonishing, but it was both!

Well, remembrances don't ever have to end, but a written compilation of them does. I leave you all with your own memories of her, and this last favorite moment of mine.

We were chatting one afternoon during one of my visits, when a therapist interrupted us. She was questioning residents at random to determine their degree of cognitive awareness. She assured me it wouldn't take more than five minutes. Did Aurore know what year this was? No. Did she know the name of the facility she lived in? No. Did she know who was president? No. She missed two more questions, smiling happily all the while. Then she reached over and gently patted the woman's knee, saying. "I'll tell you what I DO know, dear. I know that I love everyone in this place, wherever I am, and I know that they love me!"

And to that magnificent bit of wisdom, I say, then and now: "Amen!"

RIBBONS IN THE WOODS

When we were in Maine, we often played board games well into the night (especially if we had company, which was almost always!) This obviously led to much later arisings. (My mom, whose daily schedule always began at 6:00 AM, was totally discombobulated one morning to discover it was 10:30 when she awakened! She was somewhat perturbed for half a day.)

On a Friday morning one Labor Day weekend, I woke extremely early after a late game night and for some inexplicable reason, I got up and walked out to the kitchen. Drawing the curtains open, I spotted two men in the adjoining lot (which we owned) tagging trees with orange tape. A little bewildered, I got dressed and went out to investigate. In response to my questioning, the men told me they were clearing the land in preparation for a new house. "I don't think so," I said, "we own this lot." "Can't be," they answered, and added "the realtor is meeting us here in 15 minutes. Talk to her." As I sat on the porch waiting for her, I was uncomfortably checking my certainty. Our house-lot number was 2120, and we had bought 2121 as well, but as yet, there were no other homes in the entire section. All the lots were part of the forest, none of them numbered visibly. Did we own the lot in question, or the one on the *other* side of the house? This one closer to the driveway is the one we wanted for added privacy, but might we have mistakenly purchased the other one? Scary suspicions were gnawing at my composure. When a blue sedan pulled up to the site, I went to meet her. Eleanor. A pleasant lady. I felt very comfortable explaining the situation, and suggested we go immediately to the business office at Clubhouse 2, to clarify ownership. She herself had no papers with her, and ours were in RI in our safe deposit box. We left together in her car. (Everyone in the cottage still sound asleep.)

Verification proved that we were rightful owners. (Thank You, Lord!) Eleanor was totally beside herself with gratitude for the gift of having been stopped from felling trees on property that was owned by someone else. "Good grief," she moaned, "do you realize where I'd be as a realtor, if you hadn't picked up on this? That would have been the absolute end of my career! I just can't thank you enough for having checked this out. You saved me."

"Believe me, Eleanor," I responded, "it was as great a gift to us, as it was to you. This is our last weekend in Maine this summer. Had your men been working here *next* weekend, instead of this one, we would have come back at some point to our nice private wooded lot, to find it all gouged out and denuded in the center! And what could we have done about it? It would have totally desecrated our sweet little sanctuary here!" But, it *hadn't* happened!! I stopped ranting and we parted, each of us joyfully relieved!

But for Your saving grace, Lord, this would have been disastrous for both of us. I so appreciate that You woke me up and clued me in. I know it was You. Your goodness is everlasting.

DIVINE GEOMETRY

This is a fragment of a dream, many years ago.

I had died and was newly come to heaven. The Holy Trinity was there to greet me, Father, Son and Holy Spirit. They were not a threesome, a triangle, as we used to see in the catechism books, they were actually a square. I learned that the fourth corner had been vacant all this time, waiting for me ever since God had first thought of me, eons ago. I didn't know why it was that I had to spend time on earth but now I was being welcomed back by God, as the missing piece that they were waiting for.

I knew, in that dream that *every single one of us*, somehow, is that missing piece! Only a dream, but I'm glad and grateful it came to me.

Just recently, (many years after having dreamt that) I read a poem by Hafiz, a 14th century Sufi Persian poet. In it, he has God saying:

"I am made whole by your life.
Each soul,
Each soul completes me."

DOUBLE DIPPING

It was the late 1980s. Bill Bruneau and I had gone to the church bazaar in the afternoon. (George was watching a ballgame, and Bill's wife, Marie, wasn't interested in coming.) As we approached the grounds we spotted a small sailboat, (actually made of styrofoam painted green!) 9-10 ft. long with a blue sail that advertised KOOL. Obviously a promotion, and used, but just the perfect size and weight for our little lake. A bazaar worker was affixing a price tag to it. $150. She looked up at Bill and said, "We had no idea what it was worth. Do you think that's too much?" "I think it is," he replied. "I wouldn't ask for more than $100." "Well, if you left it at $150, I piped up mindlessly, I'd have no problem buying it at half-price at the end of the fair, that's for sure!" (On Sunday, everything sold for half-price, after 12:00.PM.) She turned to me and asked, "You'd buy it for $75?" "Absolutely!" I answered. "OK," she offered, "then, it's yours." I could hardly contain my elation, but I asked if she wouldn't rather wait and see if it sold at $150 first. She said, "No, a bird in the hand is worth two in the bush!" I could pay for it after the 10:30 Mass the next day, which was fine with me.

When George and I went to claim it the following morning, she told us she'd had six offers to buy it for $150. "Oh, you surely must have regretted selling it to me!" I cried, but she quickly retorted, "No, not a bit. I just figured it was your lucky day. Enjoy it!" ...and did we ever! The least little breeze would move it right along...perfect for Lake Arrowhead! We had fun in it for years, but one day, when our son was out on the lake in it, he capsized. As his head came up from the water, it poked right through the fragile sail. Disaster! I checked into replacing it with a sun-fish sail but the dimensions were off. (The $350 tag didn't seem to fit with styrofoam, either!) Looked like the wind was out of our sailing for a while...

A few days later, John MacDougall, a good friend and neighbor, stopped by for coffee. I was relating the incident to him, and added, "So now, we need a miracle! Somewhere, there's someone who had a sailboat just like this one, ruined the boat, and is left with a lonely sail." He looked at me with a weird smile and said, "I'm your man." He actually had the same craft, painted it with the wrong substance and destroyed the boat! (It was styrofoam, remember!) He came back that evening with a sail, a spare rudder, and a spare centerboard. I made sure he was to consider it "our" boat, and felt free to use it whenever he liked!

What sweet little gifts! The miracle of them both enhanced our happy sailing!

SWIMMING SOLO AT THE DAM

We had played lots of tennis that morning, and it was hot. (The tennis, *and* the weather!) When we got home, I asked if anyone was up for a dip in the lake, not at the beach, but over by the dam. No one was, so I just up and went by myself, though swimming alone is *never* a good idea.

It was cool and refreshing, and I was so glad to be there. I swam to the middle of the lake, enjoying the sheer peace and beauty around me. Suddenly, my right leg cramped hard! Calf and thigh muscles twisted agonizingly in more directions than I could keep up with. I gasped in horror, as I realized the implications. Close to despair, I turned to see how far I was from shore, and whether or not I had a chance of making it…and what did I see but the faces of Valerie and Sylvia, two of our daughters, swimming toward me, pushing a float that I would be able to cling to.

Day and night, at any given moment, You are my Savior.

A REVELATION

My reaction to her disturbed me. I was meeting the three-year-old sister of my daughter's new friend. A surprisingly unappealing little one. I've never applied that adjective to a child, but she did, in fact, unsettle me a bit. It was the vacuum in her eyes. They seemed completely lifeless. When they left, she stayed in my mind. It was distressing to me that I, who had six children at the time, and was normally attracted to little tykes, could look upon a three-year-old with even a hint of repellence.

What was wrong here? What a lonely little thing she must be, I mused, not to be attracting the oohs and aahs and complimentary comments that little ones usually elicit. The more I thought about her, the more I resolved to make up for this morning's lack of interest on my part, whenever I saw her again.

A few days later, she and her sister reappeared. "Hi, Jeanie," I said, bending down to her level. "What a pretty sweater you're wearing! It matches your eyes perfectly!" She smiled, very shyly, in response. "You look beautiful today," I continued, and hugged her. She followed her sister to another room, but with her happy eyes on me as long as possible. I felt much better myself, and mentally planned to give this little girl extra attention every time I saw her.

A week later, the two were back. Jeanie walked right up to me, and tugged at my jeans. "Know what, Mrs. Picard?" she whispered to me, as I bent over, "I love you."

The magic of love!

POETRY

At one time in my life, I discovered that poems were coming to me rather frequently... and I always got a little heads up beforehand. I just seemed to know when one was stirring within. It was a fascinating venture, and I appreciated them, as gifts. They were little bits of truth, and a source of great comfort to me.

Once, at a "Literary Arts Afternoon" at a local retirement home, fifteen aspiring but unknown Rhode Island writers, (me included) had been invited to share their work with the residents and their guests. After the reading, two very enthusiastic gals came up to me, each hoping to buy a book of my poems. When they realized there were none in print, because I was as yet unpublished, they immediately wrote their names and addresses on paper, and asked to be notified as soon as the books were available. Vitally encouraging, to say the least! But life kept getting busier...

Another day, a friend with whom I had shared several pieces, invited me to do a poetry reading at her Garden Club luncheon. It was in a private home, and there were so many members in attendance, that I had to stand between the living room and the adjoining sun-room to read to both locations—*not* a guest speaker's choice, for sure! But, the habit of doing the best you can, with whatever you have, is a very accommodating and reliable characteristic to possess. (I'm grateful to whomever I learned that from. It stands me in good stead often.)

When the presentation was over, a lovely little elderly lady came up to me, and introduced herself. She had recently moved to the state, and was on the board of the RI Historical Preservation Society, as she had been in Connecticut. "I don't think you have any idea of what just occurred here," she said, slowly and seriously, to me. "I go to a lot of lectures, and I give a lot of them, myself, so I know what I'm talking about! Well...all the time you were speaking...not one person in this living room touched her hair...or crossed her legs...or shifted position...or looked away from you! You had them totally mesmerized! That *never* happens, I can tell you!" she insisted. Her comments were thrilling to hear. (They confirmed for me what I had suspected, that some of those poems were, in fact, inspired!)

One evening, I read for the nuns at the Abbey...the most perfect audience! (I felt they enjoyed my poems and understood them as well as I did.) A year later, George and I were at a reception there, and one of the nuns said to me, "Are you still writing poems, I hope?" and *immediately*, a voice spoke from the back of my head, "Why would I send her more? She hasn't done anything with what I've sent her."

I have yet to address this.

CHARISMATIC MEETING

Our older son, Charl, and I had been going to a Charismatic group that met weekly at Our Lady of La Salette Shrine, in Attleboro. This particular evening, we had my sister and a friend with us. We arrived quite late, (a little embarrassing) and had to hunt separately for seats.

When the meeting was over, I happened to be by myself for a moment in the entryway, when a young man came looking for me. He confessed to me that he'd been so despondent that whole week, that he had planned to take his life that very night, at home. Then a thought struck him, that if he came to this prayer meeting, he would find something he needed to thwart his intention.

"When you walked into the room tonight," he continued, "I knew in my heart— don't ask me how—that Jesus was proving to me that He was alive and walking among us still."

Glory be to God !!

MICHAEL AND THE CUT BRANCH

George was heading out to trim some of the lower branches on the trees in the backyard. "Oh, please," I asked, pointing to the maple near the fence, "leave this lower left branch because I look right into that from the sink, OK? Meditating into green leaves when I'm doing dishes is so much more pleasant than staring into Gerry's open garage across the street." Considering how much time I spent at that sink, this greenery offered me luxurious privacy for my thoughts, and I had truly come to treasure it.

A half-hour later however, my view from that window was the ugly interior of a gaping garage. Not a single green leaf left to block it! I burst uncontrollably into raging tears, hating my husband instantly with an all-consuming fury I had never felt before. He had ignored my simple plea, and had…just arbitrarily…ravaged my private retreat! I went out, ranting and railing, to confront him. His non-apologetic indifference added fuel to the fire, and I stoked it for many days. This was a bitter rift. Of great concern to me was the fact that every time I looked out that window now, (countless hours!) the loathing took on new dimensions. I hated him for not caring, and hated myself for being non-loving and non-forgiving. Love had always been a big part of my life and I was as guilty as he for abandoning it. Yet at every glance through that window I saw only hatred in fiery embers, and I let it ignite my own fuming on a daily basis. It intensified every time.

A week later was Thanksgiving, and we had a houseful for the weekend. George and I hadn't reconciled, but I masked my revulsion masterfully, I thought, and no one was the wiser.

Paulette's husband, a burly mountainous man, approached me one morning when the others had left for a hike. "I may be out of line, here" he said tentatively, "but I know something's gone wrong with you and George." My steely control trembled. "Believe me," he continued, "this is nothing compared to what I know." (He had told me his parents fought a lot.) "Would you want to talk about it?" he asked gently. His sympathetic concern unleashed the flood gates, and I sobbed my way through the anger and heartbreak again, from start to finish. He listened, but said nothing.

Later that afternoon while clearing lunch dishes, I looked out that window. To my amazement I saw, not the depressing reminder I had come to dread, but my son-in-law, Michael. He had a heavy rope in one hand, looped over the branch above the one that George had severed. The other end of it was tied securely around a huge rock. There he was, pulling on the cord, enticing that upper branch to drop down just a little…then a little bit more…a little tug again, and just a bit more…

My heart was seeing Love in action. I literally felt it burst in gratitude, and the explosion blew out every bit of negativity associated with that incident, including my own firm focus on my husband's offense. George, himself, was totally exonerated! What a gift to both of us. With his glowing, glorious love, Michael had changed my window-view from rotten to radiant!

Thank you, Michael. Imagine what that did for my life, to have come to realize so experientially, that day, the *unbelievably transforming power* of *LOVE*.

NEON LETTERS

Bishop Louis E. Gelineau had just launched his Vision of Hope campaign. George went to the initial parish meeting for workers. I did not. He came back dismayed that so few people had shown up and mentioned that I should attend the next meeting to help out. A little annoyed, I responded that all my life I had worked on everything that the parish had ever offered and that this time, up-to-my-ears-busy as I was, I felt no obligation whatsoever to be there....and that if there were no workers, so be it. Comes a time when all the "old faithfuls" can afford to take a break, regardless of the outcome. In my heart, I felt perfectly justified in not participating.

When I went to bed that night, however, I said to God, "That's my honest heartfelt reaction, and I'm almost positive You'd agree with me, but, if You think otherwise, speak up. You'd better do it in neon letters, too" I added, "so I really get the message, because if not, I won't be there for sure."

The very next evening, we were on our way to Providence. We passed the Pastry Gourmet, newly erected at the corner of Albion and Mendon Roads. Because of an electrical deficiency somewhere, the neon letters forming "Pastry" and "Gourmet" were dark, except for two of them. Those were lit and pulsating in red neon. "GO" "GO" "GO" "GO"! I could hardly believe my eyes. "I'll be there," I sang back. "Gladly! Just had to hear it from YOU! Thanks for getting back to me!"

I love this kind of fascinating communication!

DIVINING MOMENT

One very special "happening" came to me in my late 50s, and I prize it profoundly still. (Though I had decided not to include it, *it* changed my mind.)

That marriage can sometimes be a challenge is a no-brainer, of course. No one who's married (and honest!) would question that. After five years of it, however, I realized in the depths of my heart that my husband and I would never be soulmates. Though he was intrinsically a good man, too many things that I deemed vital to my inner being were missing from our relationship. Truth be told, I felt the essence of me would disappear if the status quo continued. My heart and soul were aching for release, but there was none in sight.

In fairness to him, he wasn't failing in any of his duties or promises and he was never rude or unkind, either. How could I fault him for my earlier lack of insight? Nevertheless, to be brutally frank, the prospect of being married to him for the rest of my life was…repulsive. (I cringe here, at using this ugly word in reference to him, but for that point in time, it is unerringly accurate.) A pitiful dilemma of eternal proportions. Fortunately for me, we already had a 3 year old, a 2 year old, and a 4 month old baby. Three precious little tykes who needed both of us. There was no possibility that I might even consider sacrificing their lives for mine. Not ever.

I hadn't yet learned that there are *no* coincidences in anyone's life. (Isn't that an amazing thing to know, once you discover it? I do believe that every thread of our individual tapestries is woven—superbly—by Hand.) At some point during this quandary, I "happened" to see a Scripture passage that read: "Who loses his life for my sake, will find it." A promise!… The very promise my spirit needed, (and if you can't trust God, I reasoned, whom on earth could you ever trust?) I put all my eggs in that basket. I would do just that…offer my life to Him, and put my very best into whatever was facing me. I had absolutely no clue that was the very best thing that could have happened to me! A pure gift! Getting yourself out of the picture as you go about your business is phenomenal and the easiest and best way to achieve anything! I wouldn't see that for years, of course, but I did have sense enough even back then, to not let my predicament make a miserable mope out of me. On the contrary, to make the "loss" of my life somehow worthwhile, I planned to make my husband the happiest man in the world...or at least a candidate for that title! Two weeks later, at a party with friends, though I was in a different group I distinctly heard someone say to him, "George, you strike me as the happiest man in the world!" I *absolutely knew* in my soul that God was assuring me that I had made the right decision.

Time went on. We had four more children. Life was busy, full of challenges, and lots of fun. I was actually much happier than I had ever expected to be.

Well!...all this by way of introduction to the "special happening"!...Wow!... Sorry, but you really needed some background to understand this:

One ordinary day, late in the afternoon, a bizarre thought popped *forcefully,* from out of nowhere, into my mind. It said...that I had been gypping my husband almost all of our married life. It literally stupefied me! I didn't argue with it, or defend myself. I listened.

It showed me clearly that, to a great extent, from the beginning, I had concentrated almost exclusively on what he was lacking. (You can't give what you don't have, true.) But, had I ever taken a good look at what he *did* have? And offered me daily? He *was* wonderfully easy-going, not given to quarreling or disagreements and not critical...rather more complimentary most of the time. He relished my cooking, and praised my concoctions regularly. I was generally the disciplinarian of the kids, being a "stay-at-home-Mom," but he always supported my reasoning and decisions when and if they complained to him. He was an excellent father, himself, generous and genuine. He always saw things *as they were,* not negatively, but not through rosecolored glasses, either, (as is my tendency)... just *as they were*, unaltered by opinion, his or anyone else's. He was a master at his profession, head and shoulders above most, (as the powers-that-be in dentistry informed me privately at one time.) He enjoyed his patients, and consistently gave them all top-notch care. He was totally impervious to flattery or insult, and not ever moved a mite by either. I think he liked what he saw when he looked inward at himself... (that's how honest he was). He loved God. He dearly loved our children, and me, especially...I know.

I was spell-bound for a long minute...

There was no disputing the truth I had just been shown. He had actually been a superlative spouse for me all those years! How could I have been so blind?... And the painful realization set in that, through all those same years, though I had been a really good wife, I had never consciously and intentionally *cherished* him in my heart, as he truly deserved to be. I had, in fact, gypped my husband almost all of our married life.

Truthfully, I don't know if he was aware that he'd been short-changed. He always seemed happy to me. But shortly after I had experienced that divinely-inspired persuasion, and seriously altered my course, so to speak, his sister commented one afternoon, "There's something different about you these days, George. I don't know what it is, but you seem so much more positive than ever before. What's up?" I took it to be God's reassurance one more time.

I *do know* that if that powerful conviction had come to me *after* his death, and I weren't able to make amends, I would have spent the rest of my life in frenzied remorse, trying to forgive myself. Can you imagine how *grateful* I am, and *will be forever*, that my eyes were opened to my blindness?

A clinical addition;

A friend's daughter, who had been George's patient all her life, married and moved to another state, where she participated in a dental health survey. She phoned her mother that the dentist who examined her was in wide-eyed wonderment at the beautiful work in her mouth. Awestruck, he asked her permission to call in his colleagues. "Kathy," he pleaded, "we hardly ever see this level of perfection. Please, would you let them come view it?" Six dentists, she related, peered into her mouth two at a time, ooh-ing and aah-ing at all they saw, and voicing their astonishment and approbation lyrically. I appreciated that her mother saw fit to share that narrative with me. George just smiled on hearing it.

A PUZZLER

It was a special holy day. To celebrate it, our pastor had decided to offer Holy Communion under both species at that Mass. There would be a ciborium holding the hosts and two chalices on each side aisle. I was holding the second chalice on the right side. Far fewer people than we expected came to drink the Blood of Christ, and only one person had come to me. When communion time was over, Father said to those of us with a chalice, "Please consume what is in your vessel." A shock to hear, as mine held easily over two cups. I drank them, considering it a special gift, but praying to understand whatever hidden significance accompanied it. (I was reminded of Edna St. Vincent Millay's poem with the line about the saints "who, to the windows run, to see the littler tippler leaning against the sun!")

Two weeks later, at a conference in a Catholic college nearby, our small group was privileged to have a private Mass said for us on Saturday morning. At communion time, the celebrant asked for a Eucharistic Minister* to assist him. I was the only one available. He held the ciborium and handed me a full chalice. Déjà vu flooded my memory instantly, and again, very few people approached me. When we returned to the altar I knew what Father was going to say, and he did, "Please consume what's in your vessel." "What's this all about, Lord?" I asked silently. Standing with my back to the congregation, I slowly drained the entire chalice of the Blood of our Savior—and simply and seriously sought, not to understand, but to be still and just to believe that I AM is.

I continue to hope for some enlightenment concerning these two precious, but bewildering consecutive experiences.

*Now referred to as an Extraordinary Minister of Communion.

PIP PUTS THE LIGHT ON

My Dad, Pip, as we called him in later life, was always exhorting me as a child to put the light on, because I often read or worked past daytime into twilight or darker, without becoming aware of the difference. He did this very often throughout my younger years. "You're going to tear your eyes out, you crazy girl!" is what he'd say…and he said it often.

One night, years after he had left this world, I was crossing to my side of the garage, in the dark. Pitch black! I knew my way perfectly, but the thought of my Dad came to me. In deference to his sweet memory, I reached out and flipped on the light switch, though I had only a few steps more to take to reach my car.

Had I not done that, my very next move would have been to stumble over the lawn-mower, sitting where it didn't belong.

Pip, I can hardly believe you're still at it!! (I actually enjoyed the quick trip back to being eight years old again, and *hearing* your voice!) Thank you so much for sparing me a few beautiful bruises…and, quite possibly, a broken bone! I love you, Pip, and am eager to see you again.

AN UNWRAPPED WEDDING GIFT

We were in College Park, Maryland for Charl and Ania's wedding. I was in the bathroom putting on make-up. For some strange reason, I noticed that I was standing on the third tile from the baseboard, one up from the front of the sink. The very thought made me chuckle to myself, astonished that something so outlandishly meaningless should even enter my mind on such a glorious day, just perfect for their wedding.

Suddenly, there was a knock at the outside door adjacent to the bathroom. In the two seconds it took to open the door and greet Joss, who was all dressed and ready, we heard an infernal racket coming from the room I had just left. We found that a large square of heavy metal, covering electrical connections high on the wall, had broken off and fallen to the floor. It landed on the third tile from the baseboard, one up from the front of the sink.

That would have been a heavy load on my head, Lord, and I would probably have missed, and messed-up their wedding. Thank You, infinitely much, as always, for Your spectacular attention to such details.

A TEA PARTY

Phyllis was a friend of my mom's and she now belonged to our parish. She and her husband, both elderly, had recently fallen on hard times, health-wise, but happily, new friends in this area were helping with marketing, errands, and transportation to appointments, etc. She was really a sweetheart, and I loved that she had loved my mom so much. When her husband, Walter, spent time in rehab after surgery, she asked to be able to stay at the facility with him. It was allowed, and they spent several weeks together there, before he died. At that point, she decided to spend the rest of her days in the nursing home.

Whenever I passed the street that led to her new lodgings, I promised myself that I would stop and visit, but life is really busy, and it's so hard to keep abreast of everything that time after time, I drove right by. One morning, however, I did stop. On my way to her room, I had to pass through the "common room" that was filled with vacant-eyed residents in wheel-chairs, staring into space, seeing nothing and no one. Most of them were drooling. My heart lurched in my chest at such a distressing scene.

Phyllis was writing thank-you notes when I arrived, but seemed happy to take a break and chat. "Phyllis," I said, determined to get her out of there for a time, at least, "how about coming to spend tomorrow afternoon with me?" "Oh, Jackie," she protested immediately, "I know you're much too busy for that but I'm so glad you came!" "Listen," I retorted, "I'll call Simone and Terry and Rita and we'll have a tea party. It will be fun!" These ladies had all helped her out in various ways in the recent past. The suggestion brought a huge smile to her eyes, and appealed to both of us, so we planned on it for the very next day.

All the gals were happy to come. Rita picked Phyllis up at the nursing home and brought her over. I had made a pretty centerpiece and a fancy-looking ice cream cake, and we had such a delightful time…like youthful, silly schoolgirls! She was enjoying herself to the hilt, and so were we. She was still on cloud nine, wreathed in smiles, when Terry drove her back with flowers for her room, and the promise that we would meet again in two weeks. I was thanking God that our tea-party had been such an uplifting, loving source of comfort and celebration for her!

Two days later, I thanked Him again, even more profusely, when I learned she had died the previous night, in her sleep.

LET THERE BE LIGHT

I was coming down the staircase one day, when I spotted an incredible glow emanating from the den. On alert, I hurried there, and saw that the origin of it was from the adjoining kitchen.

That entire space was engulfed in the brightest, most luminous and glorious light I had ever seen. Ever! The entire room was filled with it, bouncing back and forth from walls and ceiling, surrounding me with a radiance shining so powerfully it blinded my sight. Never in my life had I been in such a fiery brilliance! The glare everywhere disguised its source. Then, I knew it was related to God, somehow.

Shading my eyes, I inched my way to the area most intensely ablaze, the window above the sink. There, on the sill, was a metal circle, the discarded cover of a tin can! What can you think of that's more useless than the cover of a tin can, once removed? But there it was…and at a glance from the sun, that worthless piece was saying, "Yes, let there be light," and became the source of that incredibly extraordinary illumination!

My take:

No matter the insignificance of the element, (you or me, for instance,) a glance from the Son, given the same positive response, might create a similar stupefying enlightenment! Worth thinking about…

When my husband, George Picard, made his "return trip" he was 85 years old, still treating dental problems every weekday but Wednesday, his life-long day off, still loving what he did.

An egg-shaped growth on his shoulder one day sent him to the doctor, and soon after, to our first oncology appointment. In previous discussions, as we considered probabilities that the future might hold, we had both decided that should the need for chemotherapy arise, we might seriously consider forgoing it. More than a few friends and acquaintances taking that route seemed to have simply prolonged their lives with nothing more than agony and anguish. At this initial encounter, we were stunned to hear the doctor say to him, "George, you have no idea how critically ill you are. We have to admit you this very afternoon and do a few tests." Then he mentioned that chemo might add a little more time and be beneficial, but the prognosis, as it stood, was maybe four months. A bit of a shock, but we're both strong believers in Divine Order…and no one lives forever…so this wasn't something we couldn't deal with.

When I returned to the hospital the next morning, Jocelyne, our youngest daughter, was with me. George's doctor came in shortly afterwards, and spoke very frankly. "You have fourth stage cancer in five places in your torso," he said. We asked the same question simultaneously, "Has this cancer been there for years, with never a symptom?" "No," he replied, "this cancer is barely three and a half months old…but voracious! The most ravenous lymphoma we have ever seen. We saw damage even overnight. Forget the chemo. Nothing will stop this. You have maybe two months."

Jossi contacted all her siblings. George came home on Saturday, December 8th, feast of the Immaculate Conception…comforting, somehow. Sylvia had come right up from NY, and surprisingly, every one of our seven children was there in two days. No spouses or grandkids with the one exception of Valerie's husband, Gary, a minister with the Way International. The only reason they were free to join us on such short notice was that they had reserved that time for a cruise to celebrate their 35th wedding anniversary. Divine Order.

Charl had brought a book of jokes with a full chapter on dental deviltry. We were constantly belly-laughing together, which I suspect was Divine Order as well. George himself was thoroughly compelling when he talked of this new chapter in our lives that he said did *not* call for tears and mourning, but for an amplitude of thanksgiving in our hearts, for grateful recognition of the exultingly happy life we had shared, and the all-encompassing Love that God had surrounded us with all those years. He was eloquent and powerful. He voiced the truth and convinced us easily that he would still be in God's comforting care for the next leg of his journey. He seemed to have no concerns—only the utmost confidence. (For months afterwards, when the kids called, they would say "Mom, wasn't that the sweetest time with Dad? He turned our sadness into warm and loving gratitude." True.)

Early Tuesday afternoon, while George was still with us, we'd all been engaged in a fascinating conversation with Gary on biblical numerology. Among other things we learned, was that the number 12 is highly significant in the realm of spiritual computing…twelve apostles, twelve tribes of Israel…also, in other realms, twelve signs of the zodiac, twelve months of the year. It seemed to be considered universally, a symbol of Divine Order. Interesting. Afterwards, I took George to our room to nap, and kissed him before I left. He held my face right up to his, and said slowly: "You and I were made for each other." My heart thanked God that I was on that same page! Those were his last words. When he woke from his nap, he was no longer lucid.

Jocelyne had previously ordered a "voice quilt" for her dad, as a Christmas present.

It was a simple recording of individual greetings from family, relatives, and friends who'd been informed of his condition, (a last hello, goodbye, Christmas greeting, funny incident, favorite memory...whatever anyone wanted to share with him before he left.) She had just received it that day, approximately seventy-five responses that would be incorporated into a "souvenir box." Sylvia immediately suggested that the messages be downloaded onto her computer so that we could play them for him that same night. We did...as we all sat around the room, some of us on the bed with him. Though he wasn't responding to us in any way, we *knew* he understood what he was hearing, because he reacted to Paulette's recorded words, raising his arm and returning her "hello" with a "hi" of his own, and a wave of his hand. We were so thrilled to *see* that, and to know he heard every word! (The last thing to give out, nurses say, is hearing, even for patients in a coma.) Well, no sooner had that "voice quilt" ended, than Joel and Sarah, Paulette and Helene returned from the Picard dental-office Christmas party. It was held that year in the mansion across from the abbey. George had absolutely forbidden them to cancel it, when they were about to. They brought him 45 personal hand-written notes from the nuns he had served so well for 50 years...and we read him every one!

He died the next day, without having regained consciousness. No matter. We were euphoric that his heart and soul had been filled with expressions of fondness and friendship, of endearment and affection, filled with Love to accompany him on his way home. It was the feast of Our Lady of Guadaloupe, whose shrine in Mexico we had visited together. That, too, was comforting. During the day Gary noted, "Do you realize that he died on the 12th day of the 12th month in the year 2012? After our conversation of the day before, we were absolutely dumbfounded! In a call to his wife, Ania, Charl had mentioned this to her. When she later asked at what time he had died, and heard at 6:42 PM, she exclaimed, "Oh my gosh, Charl, that's another 12!"

His funeral was scheduled for Monday, December 17th. That it happened to be a grand-daughter's birthday had eluded me. Her mother called to say how unhappy Emma was about it. We hadn't yet made it official, so I immediately offered to schedule it for the following day. That solved the problem. When her father heard about it, however, he took her aside, explaining that it wasn't proper to alter plans already in place just to suit her own personal wishes. "Gramps won't mind that your birthday party is the same night," he said, "He knows that was planned ahead, too!" When I heard this, it was my turn to be uncomfortable. I envisioned her being annoyed at his correction, and not very willing to do as he suggested. I hoped she'd not be resentful, but I said nothing. Later that evening, he told me she had left a note on his pillow before she went to bed, apologizing for her behavior and thanking him for his intervention. It was a response that I treasured, especially from one so young…and then I realized it was her 12th birthday!

Four years later, I was relating this account to a new, recently widowed friend, as I was driving her to an appointment. I slowed down to let a car pull out from a side street. The license plate read GP 12 .

FLAME IN THE EUCHARIST

It happened in the chapel, during the consecration at Mass. The Host that Father Hunt held up had a burning flame in it, which was actually flickering and swerving, as real flames do, and had a smaller blue one inside it. It was live, and breathtaking! Though it astonished me, I thought immediately that it must be a reflection somehow of one of the candles on the altar. I was remembering that Jesus had "appeared" to me once, on a new ring, when I was a youngster. I figured out afterwards that it had been a reflection of the stained glass window behind me. I'm sure that's what prompted my instantaneous reaction. The moment passed.

The next day it happened again. That was my wake-up call. The flame in each of the holders on the altar is a tiny little thing, barely there. This one, like yesterday's, was the whole center of the Host, and flaming intensely in 3D. I realized that it was not a reflection. What could it be but a representation of God's fervent love for us?... the kind of miracle we miss every day. Let him who has eyes, see ?...

I was—and am—sorry that I had been so ready to doubt the possibility that You were showing me something extraordinary. It was *not* a reflection of the candle on the altar. I know it was a symbol of Your wondrously immeasurable love that burns and yearns for each of us. I'm blessed and grateful to have seen it, and especially, to have had You repeat it for me! In the name of everyone, Lord, thank You for that love.

NEIGHBORS

A dear friend of mine in Maine confided this story to me recently. She had never alluded to it before.

"About 36 years ago, when John and I first moved here," she related, "I had been pleading earnestly with God for some time, to let me see His face. I had prayed for it again that morning. A little while later, Jackie, you stopped by to say hello, and to introduce yourself. Ours were the only two houses in this area, at the time. While we were chatting on the porch, all of a sudden your face was completely covered with a kind of super-imposed image of the Cross. I looked for a few minutes, trying to understand. This had nothing to do with you and me," she continued. "I think the Spirit in me was recognizing something that your Spirit was telling it: that God, in fact, truly lives and operates in anyone willing to let Him. He wears any face He can, and loves from there."

"All these years," she said, "that helped me invite Him, on a daily basis, to live and love through me."

Carolyn, thank you so much for sharing this story...from which may well ensue a beautiful influx of similar invitations. I hope so!

HAPPY HOMECOMING

Two years after George died, I decided to look for smaller housing. Much as I loved our Hadde Ave. home, it was seriously more space than I needed. I could almost sense, too, that our house would be happier with a new little family to host and harbor. I started searching. After having seen 17 condos, none of which was the least bit appealing to me, I called my realtor, Mary McNally (a good friend, by now.) "Put me on hold for a few months please, Mary," I said. "If a corner unit becomes available at Maplewoods, I'll take a look, but I don't want to see anything else for a while." Over the phone that same evening, our daughter Valerie commended me. Her exact words: "Mom, that was the absolute best thing you could have done! You know how much God loves you. He doesn't want you worrying about where you're going to live... He's preparing the perfect spot, and He'll deliver it, too." Sweet comforting words with a prophetic nuance that got by me completely. Two days later, Mary phoned. "A corner unit just showed up this morning. Want to look?"

As I crossed over the threshold of that condo, I felt literally embraced—a kind of quiet welcoming hug—and right there, in that little foyer, before seeing any separate rooms, I *knew* I was home. And no wonder! It was a near replica of the ground floor of our family home. (Not kitchen, dining and living space in one single room, as in most condos, but a room for each of those places!) A closet by the front door, (unheard of, elsewhere!) and one by the back door as well, (am I dreaming?) A spacious pantry! A bedroom that really needed our king-sized bed which, for all its sweet memories, I did not want to give up. No second floor, no basement, but more storage space than I'd seen anywhere! A porch the size of the one I was leaving and a beautiful wide front and side yard to boot, with trees and greenery my private, peaceful view from every window. What a heavenly spot!

I was delirious, and then it dawned on me that if I were a wiser woman of the world, I might comment negatively on a few things, and try not to look so delighted with all I saw… just in case my overt elation be translating to an inflated fee. (I am not usually wise in the ways of the world, but I really appreciated that this little tidbit of advice had come to me, and used it.) I made an offer that day which was accepted.

For some reason, buyers and sellers are not supposed to meet until the closing date, yet at our next appointment the owners were still at home—a sweet elderly couple with whom I connected immediately. We sat and chatted for a few moments. "I don't know if this would interest you, dear," the woman said, "but we have a friend who is a Catholic priest, and when we bought this place 20 years ago, we had him dedicate it to the Sacred Heart of Jesus." I totally understood and savored anew the warm welcome of the previous day. What a significant gift! And of course, it followed that my furnishings, full of loving history, fit perfectly in every room, including the drapes, and the handsomely colored, cherished Chinese oriental rug that has been in our family since I was four years old! Still beautiful! Many of our grandkids, on visiting, remarked, "Mimmi, it's like you brought Hadde Ave. over here with you!" And that's just how I feel—completely at home—thanks only to You.

Wherever You are, I AM, I'm completely at home. I pray that You help my siblings, all over the world, come to realize how much You love *them, personally,* and how much You'd like to do for them. Your goodness is overwhelming!

FINALLY

So... here we are, in the present moment. I really appreciate having lived this long, because, though I'm not as sharp as I used to be, (or thought I was!) I do feel a wee bit wiser...and I see that it can take years, sometimes, to get the whole picture! It's also very humbling to have spent a lifetime receiving innumerable gifts and favors like these, and to have accepted them with only minimal acknowledgement along the way...even, at times, to have forgotten about them completely. (I think I'm trying to atone for that, with these revelations!) What moves me about these stories is that reading them makes me feel special to God. They've *taught* me that I *am* special to God...but not one whit more special to Him than *you* are!...*You*...reading this! And we're both as much loved as St. John the Baptist or St. Catherine of Siena. (You might just not realize it yet.)

I thank God, profusely, for having stimulated my consciousness these later years, that I recognize more fully — though not conclusively — how thoroughly committed He is, to every one of us, right to the end! Hard to wrap your head around that, isn't it? I agree. It's almost inconceivable to our small minds that the God of all creation could love *each* of us so personally...and shower us so consistently with His blessings...but He does. *Yet*...not *ever*, not even in the *slightest* degree ever, will He *impel* us to love Him. Our response is totally, freely, up to each individual one of us. Doesn't that take your breath away?...

What an incredible adventure life is!

As a youngster, I absolutely reveled in fairytales and often envisioned, wistfully, having a fairy godmother of my own. Euphoria! Decades later, it dawned on me that I am, in all reality, living that enchanting dream of my youth. I *am* a lively, loving and much-loved participant in the one single story that eclipses all others...the *only* tale worth telling, throughout the ages.

Once upon a time......long, long ago......two souls, created by God and meant to live *with Him in joy and peace forever, were banished from Eden because of their own willful* *transgression. The original parents of humankind. Since then, an arbitrary number of years* *has been allotted to each successive soul—us!—to find our way back to Him. (Somewhat* *suggestive of an ethereal, transcendental fairytale, no?) The wicked ogre is always a threat,* *but we're promised, if we follow God's directions, an everlastingly rapturous reunion with* *Him—an eternity of bliss and beauty with our Beloved—us, beloved from before beginnings* *and borders, and beyond boundaries. Because He loves us, and wants to help us find our way,* *He sent prophets, and even gave us a manual to live by. Centuries later,* still *not giving up on* *us, He sent His Son to earth as a human being like ourselves, to save us, both of them knowing* *full well the Son would be massacred and crucified by the demonic powers there be, for* *wanting to show us how to live forever.*

You know the rest of this story, and its *glorious* sequel... Could you ever have imagined such an extraordinary destiny being offered to the original dust of us? Unreal, almost! But faith is what emboldens you to believe it, mind, heart, and soul! Aren't you excited, and grateful, that we each get to write our own personal ending to this story? We respond to LOVE or we refuse to. *Our call.* Sounds simple, doesn't it?....but, please, let's all pray for one another, and for everybody in the world, that we get it right! With God's grace, we can!

The END

(No!.....The Beginning..)

P.S. I earnestly wish for each one of you a happy, fruitful life, and a grateful core.

I leave you one of my poems to thank you for having read DIVINING MOMENTS. It's my fervent hope that some tiny seed somewhere in these pages, (maybe meant especially for you!) falls into your heart and sprouts.

WITHIN ME

Within me
Is the breath God blew
That called to life
Adam's immobility,
Made new-formed Eve delight
In what she might discover,
There in Eden,
With her lover.

Within me
Is the breath God blew.
Creative Power that He is,
This breath of His
Is substance of my own,
And though my bone be sod,
The spirit that is me
Is God.

Within me
Is the breath God blew,
Ancient as Abraham,
New as...you!

This poem begged to be included.

It was originally meant to be hand printed, enhanced a little with watercolor, framed, and when the time comes, set beside me in my coffin or by my urn. An absolute last word to all my loved ones. (And now, that includes you!)

CELEBRATE

Sing at my wedding
But dance at my death,
Drink to the end of the strife.
Pluck your guitars
And pass out cigars,
A little girl's just come to Life!

Made in the USA
Middletown, DE
18 August 2019